JOB SEEKING ON SOCIAL MEDIA

Using LinkedIn, Twitter and
Facebook to find your dream job

Written by Noé Spies
Translated by Rebecca Neal

Coaching 50MINUTES.com

LINKEDIN, TWITTER AND FACEBOOK AS JOB SEARCHING TOOLS — 1

LOOKING FOR A JOB USING SOCIAL MEDIA: THE BASICS — 3

Be visible, active and involved

Build up your network

Research companies

Get recruiters' interest

Avoid common mistakes

Social media is changing job interviews

TOP TIPS — 19

FAQS — 21

Which social networks should I sign up to?

Which social networks do I have the best chance of being seen on?

Are all social networks free services?

What should I do if I have not had a social media presence until now?

Will just using social media a lot help me to get a job?

Are recruiters really going to look at my profiles on social networks?

What is a digital reputation?

OVER TO YOU — 24

FURTHER READING — 26

LINKEDIN, TWITTER AND FACEBOOK AS JOB SEARCHING TOOLS

- **Issue:** how can I use social media to my advantage when searching for a job?
- **Uses:** by optimising your use of social networks, you will increase your chances of finding a position in the short term.
- **Context:** job searching
- **FAQs:**
  - Which social networks should I sign up to?
  - Which social networks do I have the best chance of being seen on?
  - Are all social networks free services?
  - What should I do if I have not had a social media presence until now?
  - Will just using social media a lot help me to get a job?
  - Are recruiters really going to look at my profiles on social networks?
  - What is a digital reputation?

Have you finished your studies and got your degree? Are you currently out of a job and wanting to find a new one as quickly as possible? Or are you looking for a career change by moving into a new profession? If you are currently in any of these situations, you will logically have to go through the job search process.

However, the days when it was enough to send your CV and cover letter to a potential employer are over. Nowadays, many recruiters are not satisfied with just reading your CV, but also go looking for information about you on social networks, such as LinkedIn, Twitter and Facebook. Their aim is to find out more about you, your activities and your personality.

It is therefore vital to pay attention to how you come across on these social networks when you are looking for a job. You should be present and active on them, but not in any old way! This guide will give you effective plans to optimise your presence on the three most widely used social networks – LinkedIn, Twitter and Facebook – in order to hold the attention of recruiters.

LOOKING FOR A JOB USING SOCIAL MEDIA: THE BASICS

Social networks are a mine of information about your personality. The image you display on them can be seen by your friends, of course, but also by recruiters. However, during their job search, many jobseekers neglect their presence on these sites, which in this day and age can be a fatal mistake. Conversely, if you manage to get the most out of your Facebook, Twitter and LinkedIn profiles, you could score major points with your employer before you even reach the interview stage! These are fantastic tools to develop your professional network and create new opportunities. Make sure that you enhance your presence on them.

This guide will give you some basic rules, as well as tips and tricks to apply to your social media use. The goal is to showcase a positive and professional image of yourself. Your chances of finding a job will certainly increase, whereas neglecting this aspect could put you at a disadvantage compared with other candidates.

BE VISIBLE, ACTIVE AND INVOLVED

One of the major mistakes that many jobseekers make is simply not being visible enough online. Nowadays, however, it is essential to sign up to the major social networks when you are looking for a job. We are not recommending that you reveal everything about your personal life, obviously, but rather that you show that you are sociable and professionally involved. Do not wait until the end of your studies to start. This takes time; you should therefore try to be active throughout your education or training, and maintain at least a minimal level of activity afterwards.

Social networks give you the option to control a wide range of privacy settings. Consequently, you have no excuses: displaying something or revealing a piece of information on social media implies that you want everybody to see it – including recruiters!

- On Facebook, you can decide whether or not your photographs and statuses are publicly visible.
- The same goes for Twitter.
- On LinkedIn, it is up to you to make the description of your career path clear, relevant and attractive. But be yourself! There is no point overselling yourself, as employers will notice this during the job interview.

Being involved and active, with a view to finding a job, does not mean changing your Facebook profile picture every other day or always sharing the latest viral video that made you laugh. You need to show that you have some degree of involvement with the sector you are looking for a job in. If you studied journalism, comment on current events, share information and follow people, magazines or newspapers which interest you. If you want to become an architect, like the pages of successful architects who inspire you or of your dream architectural firms, interact with experts on specialised blogs, etc. Whatever sector you are in, show your interest and commitment!

- Interact with the companies you would like to work for

one day.

- Get involved with groups in your business sector.
- Do not hesitate to contribute by leaving opinions or comments, provided that they are constructive!

On social media, you are the only person in charge. You are the one steering the ship. Be your own ambassador! You goal should be to make yourself visible in order to build up a network. A candidate who is visible and involved in their field of work will easily gain an advantage over an inactive applicant!

BUILD UP YOUR NETWORK

This is crucial for any jobseeker, whether they are looking online or elsewhere. Obviously, social networks will not offer you a job in the blink of an eye. However, the do give you the opportunity to easily get in contact with influential people in the field you are looking for a job in, which may not be possible in the "real" world. You should seize the opportunity, then! But to achieve your goals and build up a solid network, you cannot approach it haphazardly. The next few pages will provide you with tips for creating relevant connections and getting in contact with key people more easily.

The first stage is to look for people you know: one of your teachers or a person you met during an internship, for example, or even your friends from university. In this way, you can build an initial small network of professionals, based on people you have already met.

Widen your circle

The very principle of the network will then allow you to connect with other people: your contacts' contacts, who are working in the same sector. For example, LinkedIn will suggest people to connect with based on the keywords in your profile. Of course, it would be counterproductive to blindly add everybody. Especially at the start, try to establish a circle of quality contacts.

WATCH OUT!

The biggest mistake you could make here would be to rest on your laurels. Once you have created your small network, you have to maintain it! Talk to people and offer your opinion where relevant. The more active you are, the more people in your field will see you as somebody who is motivated.

A less strict hierarchy: make the most of it!

One of the major strengths of social media is that it greatly reduces hierarchical relationships. Everyone is on an almost equal footing. This aspect is essential, because it allows you to easily get in touch with influential people and gives you the chance to talk to some recruiters!

Give and take

View your activity on Facebook, Twitter and LinkedIn as interactions which allow you to be of service to your contacts, and to receive services from them in turn. If one of your connections asks a question that you know the answer to, do not hesitate to respond to them! By establishing bonds of trust, you stand to benefit too. The trick is to maintain the contacts you have made as much as possible. Members of your network will then know that they can count on you, and they will return the favour at some point. It's a win-win situation.

RESEARCH COMPANIES

Social media is a fantastic way of showcasing your professional accomplishments, but this is not its only use! For your online activity to be effective, you must also research companies, and Facebook, Twitter and LinkedIn are extremely valuable tools to do this.

A good way to gain a strong command of current news in the area you are applying for jobs in is to look as much as possible at the Facebook pages and Twitter accounts of companies which interest you and to ask interesting questions. Even if it is not immediately visible, this work of watching and researching will pay off in the long term. You will be more capable of having relevant discussions with the contacts in your networks. You will also be more aware of the projects and organisation of companies.

It will not take a recruiter long choose between a candidate who remains in their own bubble and an applicant who is up to date with the latest news in their sector.

- On Twitter, staying up to date with your sector could not be easier! All you have to do is carry out a keyword search and you will immediately come across people or companies from your field.

- You can then get an idea of certain companies' values, so as to target them more effectively when you apply.

GET RECRUITERS' INTEREST

Building up a network and gathering information on the companies you are interested in is not everything: you should also think about catching the eye of recruiters, since your main goal is still to find a job. Here are five golden rules to help you do this.

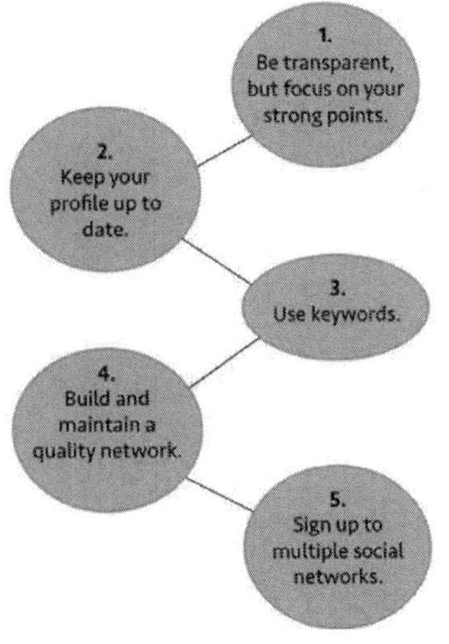

1. Be transparent and emphasise the right things

Just like writing a CV, describing your professional experiences on LinkedIn is not always easy. Above all, you must
not lie and you must not invent false experiences. Beyond
the fact that this is dishonest, recruiters can quickly check
this information, which will put you in a difficult position.
Nonetheless, being transparent does not mean saying
everything!

- Know how to emphasise relevant experiences, which
  show you in a favourable light and which will cause recruiters to judge you positively. Consequently, you should
  leave out other experiences.
- Rely on your strengths in relation to the position you are
  looking for, as this could make all the difference compared with other candidates.
- Keep your most personal information to yourself, either
  by not putting it up or by using your privacy settings.

2. Constantly update your profile

If your LinkedIn, Facebook or Twitter profiles seem to be
inactive, recruiters will question how motivated you are.
When you use social media to search for a job, you are in a
way a product, and the only ambassador for this product is
you. Social media activity is becoming increasingly similar
to marketing: you need to be able to sell yourself. To do this,
your profiles must be updated regularly.

- On the one hand, your profile will appear higher in Google
  results.

- On the other hand, it will make your presence more credible.
- By regularly updating your profile, you are positioning yourself as a professional who is in touch with reality and who pays attention to new trends in your sector. This makes your profile come alive.

On LinkedIn, you should also pay attention to your title and description in order to catch the eye of recruiters.

3. Use the right keywords

When you are describing your skills, know how to identify the most commonly used keywords in your field. It is easy to miss out some keywords which are very widely used, and therefore very widely searched for, in the sector you are interested in – it would be a shame to miss out on this advantage!

Use terms that are technical and specific to your field. When recruiters are looking for specific profiles on LinkedIn, they will never type "jobseeker" in the search bar. You must therefore think about being sufficiently precise about what you are looking for. However, do not forget to still be yourself and add a personal touch to your description, especially on LinkedIn and Twitter. Try to make yourself stand out from formatted profiles, which often bore recruiters.

- By being yourself, you will have a higher chance of receiving offers that are better suited to you, based on what you like.
- Do not hesitate to go into more detail about skills that you were unable to explain on your CV. LinkedIn offers you this additional freedom.

4. Choose your contacts carefully and talk to them!

When you are gradually building up your network, it is essential to choose your contacts carefully and avoid indiscriminately inviting everybody. To start with, connect with people you know personally and send them a personalised message, not a standardised one (which could put people off). Then, when it comes to your contacts' contacts, only invite people who put out relevant and interesting content in your field. This is how you will build a quality network. Finally, do not stop at just putting out information: comment on what other people are writing as well (but make sure you keep it relevant). Being open to other people and commenting on their activities is the only way you will forge strong relationships. Once again, you have to be active and dynamic!

5. Sign up to multiple networks

It would be a mistake to only use one social network. By expanding your presence on different networks, you will logically increase your connections and, above all, your visibility. Non-specialised networks such as Facebook, Twitter, LinkedIn and Viadeo, among others, are all excellent ways to develop contacts.

> **EXTRA INFORMATION**
>
> There are also other, specialist networks. Depending on your industry, research networks for professionals in your sector – you should find a lot of them! This will allow you to directly enter a more specific circle.

AVOID COMMON MISTAKES

In the digital era, applying online may seem very simple: you no longer need to copy up multiple hand-written letters and send them by post. It is 'enough' to take care of your reputation on social media and send cover letters by email. However, it is very easy to become apathetic and to make avoidable gaffes. Here are some mistakes to avoid when looking for a job on the internet.

Intrusive Facebook friend requests

It is good to create a network of friends on Facebook, but be careful that you do not try to add just anyone! If you have just seen a job advert that appeals to you, send a formal cover letter and CV, but do not try to add the person as a friend on Facebook. They may consider this as intrusive and inappropriate, and you may lose points with them.

- Consider Facebook as a much more personal social network than LinkedIn or Twitter. You should already know the person before making them your Facebook friend.
- Following someone on LinkedIn or Twitter can be done more freely.
- Conversely, you can 'like' the Facebook page of the company you are applying to: in this way, you will show that you are interested without coming across as intrusive. However, that will not be enough to make you stand out.

Being too insistent over email

Let's say you've just sent your CV and cover letter in response to a job posting, but after three days the recruiter still has not got back to you. Refrain from contacting them for an update too soon. The recruitment process often takes time. Sending a series of reminders is pointless, and will just make you seem impatient. If you still have not had a response two or three weeks after applying, you could contact them again to see where they are at in their recruitment process, without coming across as too pushy.

Not adjusting your privacy settings on Facebook

If you leave your photos or latest statuses public on Facebook, everyone will be able to see them. This could include photos of your last sunbathing session or your last night out, which a friend took without you knowing... To avoid revealing these parts of your private life, which are likely to make you seem unprofessional in the eyes of a recruiter, take care to adjust your privacy settings so that only your friends can see them.

TO DO

Only leave public a serious and professional image (featuring only your studies and place of birth, with a profile photo which shows you to your advantage while remaining neutral).

Putting up personal tweets

Few people think about making their Twitter profile private. Consequently, if you share how you are feeling on this social network, anyone can access it. That includes the HR director who has just interviewed you (or is going to interview you). This is the case even if they do not 'follow' you. You can certainly leave your profile public, but in this case, it is advisable to only tweet about your professional field, or at least to avoid ranting about personal issues or talking about your latest romantic encounter. Not altering the way you tweet could harm you professionally.

SOCIAL MEDIA IS CHANGING JOB INTERVIEWS

All this work of getting involved with social media as outlined above is essential, because your reputation and the way you present yourself on the internet can now guide your job interview.

- Before social media, recruiters did not have many ways of researching a candidate. The job interview was therefore the decisive stage of the recruitment process.
- Nowadays, employers can get an idea of your personality, your interests and your skills in an area before they even meet you! In other words, the employer already knows a good amount about you – provided that you are present on the social side of the internet.
- As such, social networks are changing the rules of job interviews: they allow recruiters to be more direct, to question the candidate about a specific point, to ask them about their activity on a social network, to cut right to the chase about what interests them about you, etc. This is why it is good to be involved in the right way: it will allow you to come to the interview with a definite advantage.

It is even possible to imagine that, a few years from now, job interviews will be the culmination of a relationship established through social media. But be careful not to think that the recruitment process only takes place on social networks: there is still another big hurdle to get over! Virtual exchanges will never replace in-person meetings, but they can have a major influence on them.

- Do not wait until you have finished your studies, or decided that you want a career change, to become active on social media. Get started as early as possible, and keep up your activity!
- Try Googling your name, as if you are the recruiter. Are you happy with the results that come up? What would you like to change? This is a good way of assessing yourself and becoming aware of the image that you transmit.
- Delete or make private any personal content on social media that could harm you in a job search (photos, statuses, etc.). On Twitter and Facebook, adjust your privacy settings so that you only make public a positive and professional image of yourself. To sum up: keep your private life and your professional life separate.
- Fill out your LinkedIn profile in as much detail as possible. Describe your skills, professional experiences, activities and current projects. Unlike Facebook and Twitter, LinkedIn is used for purely professional purposes, so make the most of this to be comprehensive!
- On LinkedIn, select a professional photo which fits well with the sector you are targeting. Take care with your title and description, and use the right keywords. Do not forget that this is your showcase.
- Unlike a CV, a social network allows you to include links to your activities, to a blog that you might have, to an article that you wrote, or to any other projects. This develops and strengthens what you are saying. Consequently, do not hesitate to add links to your projects in order to

illustrate your skills. These details reassure recruiters that you are presenting yourself truthfully.

- In your networks, do not hesitate to approach other people and businesses, comment, discuss generate debate, and share information and projects. This is how you will create connections and get others to approach you in turn. Always keep your contributions polite and relevant.

- Tweet professionally. Make sure that most of your tweets are focused on the sector you are targeting, or retweet messages from users or companies that you find interesting.
- React quickly to any job postings that you see on social networks. This is also a way of demonstrating to the recruiter that you are reactive. Try not to take longer than two days to respond to an advert.

FAQS

WHICH SOCIAL NETWORKS SHOULD I SIGN UP TO?

The best approach is to diversify as much as possible and therefore to at least sign up to non-specialised social networks such as Facebook, Twitter and LinkedIn. This will allow you to increase your number of contacts. You should also consider Google+ and Viadeo, and even possibly Pinterest, Instagram or YouTube, if your career plan lends itself to this.

Furthermore, it is recommended that you sign up to more specific and specialised networks depending on your field. These sector-specific networks can be useful for you, if you have a very specific profile, but also for recruiters who can carry out more targeted searching.

WHICH SOCIAL NETWORKS DO I HAVE THE BEST CHANCE OF BEING SEEN ON?

All of them! This is why it is useful to expand your presence. However, networks such as Facebook and Twitter do not have a strictly professional function. Their primary use is not for job searching. They are more for creating a network and a community, and for making your interest in a particu-lar field and your involvement in a particular project known. Conversely, LinkedIn was created for purely professional purposes. Recruiters therefore have a greater presence on it, so it should be a priority for you.

ARE ALL SOCIAL NETWORKS FREE SERVICES?

Yes, in theory. Nonetheless, LinkedIn, for example, offers users a paid service which allows them to appear higher in search results and make themselves more visible to recruiters. The same service is available for businesses to make themselves more visible to candidates. In this way, the Premium subscription allows candidate to appear at the top of the list of applicants when they apply for a job. In order to counteract this with the free version and remain high up on the list, it is very important to make good use of sector-specific keywords in your description.

WHAT SHOULD I DO IF I HAVE NOT HAD A SOCIAL MEDIA PRESENCE UNTIL NOW?

Sign up as soon as possible! Do not worry, this does not mean you will definitely miss out. However, nowadays a candidate with no social media presence can easily find themselves at a disadvantage. This absence could indicate a lack of involvement on your part, and even make you appear as someone with little interest in the world around them, thus putting the recruiter off before they have even read your CV. This is all the more true if you are in sectors like communication, journalism, marketing, advertising or audiovisual: in these industries, it is becoming almost compulsory to have an online presence.

WILL JUST USING SOCIAL MEDIA A LOT HELP ME TO GET A JOB?

Of course not! Unfortunately, there is no magic formula, unless you are very lucky. Traditional recruitment procedures are still in use. However, your activity on social media can only benefit you in the long term. It will allow you to seize certain opportunities, expand your contacts list, and therefore make a name for yourself.

ARE RECRUITERS REALLY GOING TO LOOK AT MY PROFILES ON SOCIAL NETWORKS?

It would be very difficult to prove that they all will. However, it is certain that a substantial proportion of recruiters nowadays use social networks to analyse a candidate's profile in more depth, and to dig up information before a potential job interview.

WHAT IS A DIGITAL REPUTATION?

Digital reputation simply means a person's reputation on the internet. It is the image that internet users have of a person based on their online presence. It is therefore very important that you control this reputation so that it does not incorrectly represent your personality.

OVER TO YOU

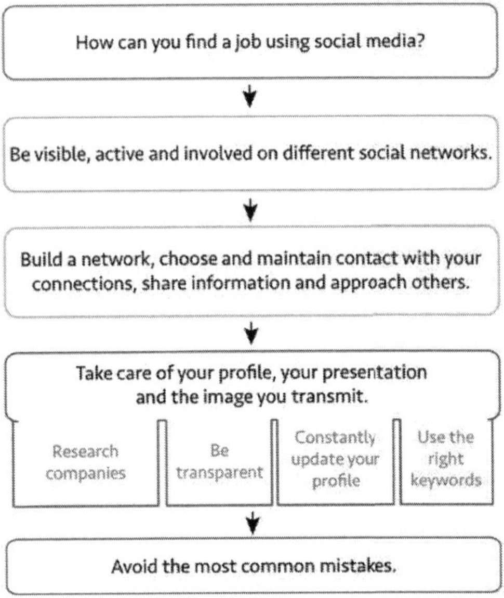
How can you find a job using social media?
Be visible, active and involved on different social networks.
Build a network, choose and maintain contact with your connections, share information and approach others.
Take care of your profile, your presentation and the image you transmit.
Research companies
Be transparent
Constantly update your profile
Use the right keywords
Avoid the most common mistakes.
Job Seeking on Social Media © 50MINUTES.com

We want to hear from you!
Leave a comment on your online library
and share your favourite books on social media!

FURTHER READING

BIBLIOGRAPHY

- Anna, J.-C. (2013) *Job et réseaux sociaux. Connectez-vous.* Paris: Hachette.
- Bréau, A. (2012) Les faux-pas fatals de la recherche d'emploi 2.0. *Terrafemina.* [Online]. [Accessed 14 November 2016]. Available from: <http://www.terrafemina.com/emploi-a-carrieres/actu/articles/13575-les-faux-pas-fatals-de-la-recherche-demploi-20.html>
- Grégoire, E. (no date) Facebook, gérer sa vie privée quand on cherche un emploi. *Cijd.com.* [Online]. [Accessed 14 November 2016]. Available from: <http://www.cidj.com/trouver-un-emploi-avec-les-reseaux-sociaux/facebook-gerer-sa-vie-privee-quand-on-cherche-un-emploi>
- Grégoire, E. (no date) Les réseaux sociaux modifient les entretiens de recrutement. *Cijd.com.* [Online]. [Accessed 14 November 2016]. Available from: <http://www.cidj.com/trouver-un-emploi-grace-aux-reseaux-sociaux/en-quoi-les-reseaux-sociaux-changent-ils-l-entretien-d-embauche>
- Grégoire, E. (no date) Se constituer un réseau grâce à Facebook, Twitter, Viadeo ou LinkedIn. *Cijd.com.* [Online]. [Accessed 14 November 2016]. Available from: <http://www.cidj.com/trouver-un-emploi-avec-les-reseaux-sociaux/se-constituer-un-reseau-grace-a-facebook-twitter-viadeo-ou-linkedin>
- Grégoire, E. (no date) Utiliser Twitter de manière pro. *Cijd.com.* [Online]. [Accessed 14 November

2016]. Available from: <http://www.cidj.com/
trouver-un-emploi-grace-aux-reseaux-sociaux/
utiliser-twitter-de-maniere-pro>
- Grégoire, E. (no date) Viadeo, LinkedIn, l'importance
du profil. *Cijd.com*. [Online]. [Accessed 14 November
2016]. Available from: <http://www.cidj.com/
trouver-un-emploi-grace-aux-reseaux-sociaux/
viadeo-linkedin-l-importance-du-profil>
- Perez, D. (2014) Cinq règles d'or pour doper sa carrière
grâce aux réseaux sociaux. *L'Express emploi*. [Online].
[Accessed 14 November 2016]. Available from: <http://
www.lexpress.fr/emploi/conseils-emploi/cinq-regles-
d-or-pour-doper-sa-carriere-grace-aux-reseaux-so-
ciaux_1573007.html>
- Perez, D. (2014) Trois conseils pour intéresser les recru-
teurs sur les réseaux sociaux. *L'Express emploi*. [Online].
[Accessed 14 November 2016]. Available from: <http://
www.lexpress.fr/emploi/conseils-emploi/3-conseils-
pour-etre-recrute-grace-aux-reseaux-sociaux_1538255.
html>

ADDITIONAL SOURCES

- Elad, J. (2016) *LinkedIn for Dummies*. New Jersey: John
Wiley & Sons.
- Macarthy, A. (2013) *How To Build the ULTIMATE
LinkedIn Profile In Under An Hour: Boost Your Branding*.
CreateSpace Independent Publishing Platform.

IMPROVE YOUR GENERAL KNOWLEDGE
IN A BLINK OF AN EYE !

www.50minutes.com